## Volume 6

# Lost In Michigan
### Tales From An Endless Road Trip

www.etaoinpublishing.com

Publisher:   Etaoin Publishing and Huron Photo LLC
             Saginaw, MI
             www.EtaoinPublishing.com
             www.HuronPhoto.com

Cover Design: Rick Ratell
              Cleaverleaf Design Services
              Midland, MI

Ordering Information:
Books may be ordered from www.LostinMichigan.net

Printed in the United States of America

ISBN 978-1-955474-05-4

Dedicated to the libraries in Michigan. From big cities to small towns, the books they contain are priceless information.

# Introduction

I have been creating posts and books for Lost In Michigan for nearly a decade. During book signings, or other events, I have overheard people make comments "Lost in Michigan, that's too funny that you can't find your way around the state. It's not that difficult." I think people still think of the stereotypical male ego of not asking for directions, especially in the modern era of GPS.

In my mind "lost" also refers to the locations and things that are lost to history and forgotten memories. It's the oddball roadside tourist trap or long forgotten building that has not been occupied in years. I know some of these places are politically incorrect or from an era that had different needs. I hope that maybe these "lost" places will be found and remembered by future travelers so their importance or memories will live on to remind future generations of what living in the Great Lakes State was like for earlier generations.

I also have to admit that I do get lost on occasion. It's not that I don't know how to read a map or work the GPS in my smart phone. It's more like I don't pay attention to where I am when I zig zag my way on the back roads. Sometimes, I end up in some small town not knowing exactly where it's located in the state. I figure I can't get too lost since I am bound to hit one of the Great Lakes or Ohio.

The locations in this volume start at the bottom of the state and then work north. Each story is independent of one another. You can read them in any order you wish. I have done my best to give an address that you can use in a GPS to help you find each location. Some places do not have an address, so I have given a description of where they can be found or coordinates for a GPS. Most locations are on public property, but some may be privately owned. Whether they are public or private, they may not be open to visitors, or they may only be open at scheduled times. Most places can be seen from public roads. I don't trespass and I advise anyone against it. Please be respectful to the places you visit. I hope after reading this book you will take an interest in traveling the back roads of Michigan and see what you can find.

# Contents

## Chapter One
## Southern Lower Peninsula

# Chapter 2
# Central Lower Peninsula

# Chapter 3
## Northern Lower Peninsula

# Chapter 4
# Upper Peninsula

# Chapter One
# Southern Lower Peninsula

# The Cannon On The Red Arrow Highway

Location:
8777 Red Arrow Hwy.
Watervliet, MI 49098

The Red Arrow Highway is a stretch of road running from New Buffalo to Kalamazoo. Originally part of US-12, the road was renamed in 1952 for the 32nd Infantry Division. In 1917, during the First World War, the division

2

was comprised of men from both Michigan's and Wisconsin's National Guard. Their insignia was a red arrow. The 32nd Infantry was once again sent into battle after the Japanese attacked Pearl Harbor and they proudly wore a red arrow patch on their uniform.

Interstate 94 is the main route through the southwest part of the mitten. It replaced the old two lane Red Arrow Highway but part of it can still be traveled. A section of it passes through the town of Watervliet. Just outside of town, an old cannon stands next to VFW Post 6803. The antique gun dates back to World War I. The wooden chassis and wheels were built by Studebaker. The barrel was made in Watervliet, New York where the United States created an arsenal in 1813 along the Hudson River. It is the oldest continuously active arsenal in the United States, and today produces much of the artillery for the army, as well as gun tubes for cannons, mortars, and tanks.

Watervliet, Michigan was named after Watervliet New York, where the first settlers to the area in Michigan came from in the 1830s. I can only assume that the connection between the two towns is how this historic cannon came to stand in the southwestern Michigan town.

# A House And The BB Gun

Location:
233 South Main St.
Plymouth, MI 48170

Next to the library in downtown Plymouth is an old brick house with a gingerbread style roof and beautiful stained glass windows. It was constructed in 1875, for Henry William Baker who helped start the Plymouth Iron Windmill Company. Early windmills were made of wood and in 1892, inventor Clarence Hamilton patented a stronger steel windmill. With windmill sales struggling because shipping the heavy windmills by wagon was a challenge. Hamilton also manufactured BB guns in Plymouth and he convinced the board of the windmill company to giveaway an air rifle as an incentive. The customers received a rifle with the purchase of every windmill.

By 1895, the air rifles were more popular than the windmills and the company became the Daisy Manufacturing Company, producing BB guns in Plymouth until 1956 when new owners moved the company to Arkansas. The Daisy Red Ryder BB gun is what Ralphie, in the movie *A Christmas Story*, asked Santa for Christmas, to which he got the response "You'll shoot your eye out, kid". The old Daisy Manufacturing Company factory in Plymouth was demolished in 2005 and a condominium complex was built in its place. The brick house with the gingerbread style roof still stands as a connection to the popular air rifle manufactured in Plymouth long ago.

General manager of the Plymouth Iron Windmill Company, Lewis Hough, test fired the gun and exclaimed, "Boy, it's a daisy!" and the name of the air rifle company was born.

# The Walker Tavern at Cambridge Junction

Location:
13200 M-50,
Brooklyn, MI 49230

Long before the automobile or train, Detroit and Chicago were both small cities among a vast wilderness of trees and swamps. Travelers used a Native American trail to travel between the two Great Lake cities. This trail became the Old Chicago Road and it took five days for people who were traveling by wagon to go from Detroit to Chicago.

Around 1832, Calvin Snell built a two story house where the La Plaisance Pike crossed the Chicago Road. He welcomed weary travelers along their journey. Ten years later Sylvester and Lucy Walker purchased the house, and renamed it the Walker Tavern. For twenty-five cents, stagecoach passengers could get a warm meal but the plates were nailed down to the table to keep them from being stolen. If you were lucky, they were cleaned between meals. For another twenty-five cents, travelers could get a bed upstairs although they may have had to share it with two other people and hope they didn't have lice.

The tavern became a popular stop in southern Michigan and in 1853, the Walkers built a larger brick tavern across the street. The old tavern was purchased in 1865 by stagecoach driver Francis Dewey. Three generations of the Dewey family ran the old tavern until it was purchased in 1922 by Fredrick Hewitt, an Episcopalian minister and antiques collector. Hewitt turned the old tavern into a museum and built a summer home on the property. After the stock market crash in 1929, Hewitt sold his home in Dearborn and moved permanently into this summer home.

The Old Chicago Road became US-12 in 1926 and the automobile became the preferred mode of transportation. To compete with the tourist traps, and other establishments that sprang up along the popular tourist route, Hewitt promoted the old tavern by embellishing some stories about it's history. He dubbed one of the rooms in the old inn "the murder room". He claimed a wealthy cattleman stayed overnight at the tavern. The next morning the man was missing and a pool of blood was on the wooden floor. The room was decorated with antiques and a blood stain could be seen on the floor. The murder was never confirmed in any documents, but the macabre story drew in motorists.

In 1965, the old tavern, Hewitt house, and eighty acres were sold to the state of Michigan. The property is now the Cambridge Junction Historic State Park. The Michigan History Center operates the tavern as a historic site during the summer.

**Trip Tip**: If you plan to visit this historic site, be sure to check the schedule for the Michigan International Speedway which is nearby. The museum is closed on race weekends because of the heavy traffic.

# The Notch of Michigan

Location:
Michigan, Ohio and Indiana
Tri-State Border
41.69645758011927,
-84.80595941372101

The southern border of Michigan has a pronounced notch where Indiana and Ohio meet up to form the border of all three states. Near the tri-state intersection is a boulder that reads:

130 feet south is the point where Indiana, Michigan, and Ohio meet. This marker was erected by the Hillsdale County Historical Society in 1977

Michigan ended up with this odd notch because Ohio, which had already become a state in 1803, refused to relinquish Toledo to Michigan. The Northwest Ordinance of 1787 established an east-west line drawn from the southern tip of Lake Michigan across the base of the peninsula. A line was drawn across a map that intersected Lake Erie north of the Maumee River. When Michigan applied for statehood in 1833, its surveyors found the line intersected Lake Erie about eight miles south of the Maumee River. The land in contention became known as the Toledo Strip.

Both Michigan and Ohio claimed ownership of the Toledo Strip. Politicians from Ohio protested Michigan's application for statehood and claimed that Toledo was theirs, knowing that it was an important port on the Great Lakes. This led to some serious altercations, including the time the Michigan Militia captured nine surveyors and arrested some Ohio officials. The feud became known as the Toledo War and although no one was hurt or injured in the so called "war", it showed how ingrained in their position each side was. In a compromise Washington D.C. decided to give Toledo to Ohio and the Upper Peninsula to Michigan and that is why the border of Ohio angles up above Toledo.

Indiana officially became a state in 1816, about twenty years before Michigan. When Indiana surveyed their northern boundary, instead of starting at the southernmost tip of Lake Michigan, they started about ten miles north in order to include several miles of Lake Michigan shoreline. In the early 1800s it was important to have access to the Great Lakes since shipping was the primary means of transportation and commerce in the region. Indiana's survey is the other reason why Michigan ended up with a notch at the southern border.

The stone, erected by the Hillsdale County Historical Society in 1977, marks the southernmost point in Michigan. Well, almost the southernmost point. I am not exactly sure why it is 130 feet from the tri-state point but the exact location is in a low spot and drops off quickly from the road. I am thinking they placed the marker at its current location because it is a nice spot on a grassy knoll. There is not a lot to see at the southern point except farmland, trees and the stone marker but it is one of those places that you can say you have visited.

It is believed that during the "Toledo War" people in Ohio began calling Michiganians wolverines as an insult because of the animal's reputation of being ornery. Michiganians thought the name was more of a compliment than an insult and that is how the University of Michigan acquired its mascot.

# The Keeper At South Haven

Location:
60 Water Street
South Haven, MI 49090

James S. Donahue rose to the rank of Captain in the Union Army during the Civil War. He lost a leg in the Battle of Wilderness and retired from active duty. In need of a job, he applied for duty as a lighthouse keeper. He was denied a position as a lighthouse keeper after the people in charge learned of his disability,. He responded, requesting that he be given a chance. The lighthouse board honored his request in 1874, and gave him the position of head keeper at the South Haven Lighthouse.

The lighthouse is a typical southern Michigan lighthouse on the Lake Michigan shoreline. The tower is at the end of a pier with a catwalk that runs the length of the pier. The keeper's house is further inland so the keeper had to walk from the house to the light at the end of the pier every day.

I think the Lighthouse Board purposely chose that lighthouse for Donahue, figuring he would not be able to make the difficult trek that was necessary to maintain the light. The 32-year-old keeper proved them wrong and held onto his job for 36 years. He made the trip to the lighthouse in all kinds of weather, from hot summer nights to the most ferocious late autumn storms when the catwalk would be covered in ice and snow while being pummeled by gale force winds. During his time as keeper, Donahue also saved over a dozen sailors' lives, rescuing them from the icy waters of Lake Michigan. A missing leg never seemed to slow him down.

The keepers house is now home to the Marialyce Canonie Great Lakes Research Library, operated by the Michigan Maritime Museum. The staff have claimed to hear strange thumping sounds and believe it is the ghost of James S. Donahue. The noise is believed to be from his crutches as his spirit roams his former home.

# Mail Order Church

Location:
McHattie Park
300 Dorothy Street
South Lyon, MI 48178

Michigan has several historic churches. Some are enormous gothic style churches with huge stained glass windows and tall steeples that reach towards heaven. Some are smaller wooden churches in rural northern Michigan where they proudly sit among nature's beauty. I

18

have seen many churches on my travels around the state. I saw this little white chapel in South Lyon that stands in McHattie Park.

I read on the sign attached to the chapel that the chapel is a Sears and Roebuck mail-order portable chapel. I was aware that Sears sold kit homes but not chapels. It makes sense now that I think about it since it is basically a house with a steeple. I guess it gives new meaning to "House of worship."

The chapel was built on East Liberty Street in 1930 and it was donated to the City by the congregation of the Immanuel Lutheran Church. In 2001 it was moved to McHattie Park. Athough it is no longer used for worship by a congregation the little chaple is rented out for weddings and other events.

McHattie Park is also home to the historic Witch's Hat Depot Museum and a few other historic buildings that were moved to the site and preserved for future generations.

# The Wing House

Location:
27 South Jefferson Street
Coldwater, MI 49036

The southern Michigan town of Coldwater has some impressive historic buildings as well as several large ornate old houses. Among them, the Wing house, on the corner of South Jefferson and East Pearl Streets, stands out with its Second Empire construction and mansard roof.

The home was originally constructed in 1875 for Jay Chandler and his new wife Francis. Jay was the son of Albert Chandler, a prominent Coldwater businessman who founded the Coldwater Sentinel newspaper and served as the city's first mayor. The design of the home was inspired by Frances' childhood home in Montour Falls, New York.

In 1882, Chandler sold the house to Civil War Captain Lucius M.Wing, who served as both Sheriff and Mayor in Coldwater. Wing and his wife Adeline made notable contributions to the industrial, financial and social life of the city. He was the long time president of the local bank. After Lucius died in 1921, the home passed through three generations of his family. The Branch County Historical Society purchased it in the 1970s and operates it as a museum to share some of the history of Coldwater.

Mansard roofs were a popular design element in France because they created more living space without having the taxation of a second floor.

# Meads Mill Ruins

Location:
Hines Park
11400 Edward N Hines Drive
Plymouth, MI 48170

Hines Park is a Wayne County park situated between Northville and Plymouth. The Middle River Rouge flows through it and you may notice an old stone structure that crosses the river. A nearby sign reads Meads Mill. It was built in 1830 and at the time was the largest flour mill in the state of Michigan. The mill burned down in 1857 and was never rebuilt.

Even though the sign near the ruins reads Meads Mill, from what I have found, it is believed that they were part of a 1937 Works Progress Administration project. The ruins were part of a waterwheel and intake site for the Wayne County Training School powerhouse. Whatever the ruins were for, it is an interesting place to visit with a nice little waterfall.

**Trip Tip**: If you want to see the stone ruins there is a small parking area off Edward M Hines Drive near the Meads Mill sign.

# Slayton Arboretum

Location:
100 Barber Drive
Hillsdale, MI 49242

On the campus of historic Hillsdale College you can find The Slayton Arboretum. It is a fourteen acre oasis with a small pond and waterfall and a plethora of plants in its gardens. In 1922, college alumni Mr. and Mrs. George A.

Slayton donated land to the college to celebrate the fiftieth anniversary of their graduation.

Biology professor Dr. Bertram A. Barber used the donated land to create the arboretum. With the help of student and faculty volunteers a pond was dug and a rock garden created. A field stone gazebo was built at the top of the hill and a pump station was added to create a waterfall. Over the decades, plants and gardens have been added along with new trails that wind through the arboretum. The arboretum is open to visitors and if you love waterfalls this is a wonderful place to visit. It may be a man-made waterfall but it is spectacularly landscaped.

**Trip Tip**: The entrance to the Slayton Arboretum is near the intersection of Barber Drive and Union Street. Two Hour parking spots are available for visitors on Barber Drive.

# Niles Train Depot

Location:
598 Dey Street
Niles, MI 49120

The southwestern Michigan town of Niles has a lot of historic architecture. Among the old houses and buildings is a beautiful stone train depot. It was constructed in 1892 and the exterior remains mostly unchanged. The depot is still used by Amtrak for passenger train service. Both the

Blue Water Train, that travels from Port Huron to Chicago, and the Wolverine Train, that travels from Pontiac to Chicago, pass through this station. It is about an hour ride by train from this station to Chicago.

The station has served as a filming location for three major films. *Continental Divide* starring John Belushi, *Midnight Run* starring Robert De Niro and James Grodin and *Only The Lonely* starring John Candy and Ally Sheedy had scenes filmed at the station. During the filming of *Only The Lonely* the station was decorated with Christmas lights and the tradition of illuminating the station for the holidays has continued every year since.

John and Horace Dodge were born in Niles, Michigan and honed their machining and engine building skills in the southwestern town before moving to Detroit to manufacture automobiles.

# The Ruins At Haven Hill

Location:
Haven Road
Highland State Recreation Area
White Lake, MI 48383

Edsel Ford purchased land west of Pontiac in Highland and White Lake Townships in the early 1920s. The property contains one of the highest points in Oakland County. It was on this hill that Edsel Ford built a massive

28

log lodge in 1923. The lodge known as Haven Hill was a popular retreat for the Ford family and their distinguished guests which included Thomas Edison, Charles Lindbergh and actor Jackie Cooper. The estate included a log carriage house, pool, riding stables, tennis courts and a toboggan run with a motorized lift.

After Edsel's death in 1943, his wife Eleanor sold the estate to the state of Michigan to be used as a state park. The state used the buildings as visitor centers until budget cuts forced the park to close them. Tragically the massive lodge was destroyed by arson in 1999.

Some of the foundation, stonework, and part of a stone chimney are all that remain of the once glorious lodge. Circular stone markers are placed to note where the different rooms were once located. Some of the other structures including the carriage house still stand but are closed to visitors. It is a fascinating site to walk around imagining what once was.

> **Trip Tip:** It is about a half-mile hike uphill most of the way to the ruins of the lodge. It is not too difficult, but plan on taking some time to make the climb.

# House of Eights

Location:
57500 Van Dyke Ave.
Washington, MI 48094

During the summer of 1828, Loren Andrus came to
Michigan from New York with his family as a young boy.
By the time he reached his twenties he was a surveyor for
the Clinton-Kalamazoo canal. In the 1850s, the more

prominent residents of Washington Township began building opulent homes to show off their wealth.

In 1858, Loren Andrus commissioned his brother-in-law and architect David Stewart to construct a home for his family. The home's design was inspired by Orson Squire Fowler's book *A Home For All* where the octagon shape was touted for its ability for natural lighting and easier to heat in the winter. Andrus' two-story Italianate home was made from local materials and took two years to construct. It became known by the locals as "The House of Eights."

Andrus, his wife, and their eight children lived in the house where they frequently entertained guests. They were active in social organizations and often held parties and receptions in their home. The house was also rumored to be a stop on the Underground Railroad.

Loren's wife Lucina died in 1890 and four years later he sold the house and moved to Detroit to live with his daughter. The house changed hands a few times. It was used as a restaurant in the 1930s and in the 40's the home and property were used to train high school students in farming and agriculture. It was eventually sold to Wayne State University in the 1950s where it became an extension of their Agricultural College. The college sold the property and after a few more owners, and years of neglect it became dilapidated and in need of renovation. It was slated for demolition in the 1980s but was saved from the wrecking ball when it was purchased by William and Phyllis Hamilton who restored the home. Currently the home is owned by Friends of the Loren Andrus Octagon House.

You can find out how to visit the home at their website www.octagonhouse.org. If you are into ghost hunting, a tour is led by the Motor City Ghost Hunters.

# Chapter Two
# Central Lower Peninsula

# Circus Train Disaster

Location:
8750 East Prior Road
Durand, MI 48429

South of Durand, in a rural area of Shiawassee County, is the Lovejoy Cemetery. Near the western entrance of the cemetery is a tall slender obelisk that marks one of Michigan's deadliest train accidents.

On August 6th, 1903, two trains from the Wallace Bros. Circus traveled from Charlotte, Michigan to Lapeer. The first train stopped in Durand at 8:30 in the morning and put up a red signal to alert the second train. When the engineer of the approaching train applied the brakes, they failed. Realizing that a collision was inevitable, the engineer and fireman both jumped from the locomotive seconds before the impact. The crew and performers in the first train were completely unaware of the situation that was unfolding behind them. The second train crashed into the rear of the first train with tremendous force.

The wreck injured about one hundred people and calls rang out for local doctors to help with the wounded. A makeshift hospital was made in the hotel downtown. Twenty two people died in the accident and another four people died in a hospital in Detroit after being transported there by train. Several animals were also killed, including an Arabian horse, three camels, one great dane and an elephant named Maud. They were buried in a field at the impact site.

After the wreck, a temporary morgue was set up so the families of the victims could identify and claim the body of their loved one. Some of the bodies were so badly disfigured that they were not recognizable and therefore could not be identified. Ten of the unknown corpses were buried at Lovejoy Cemetery, a few miles south of Durand. A stone obelisk was erected and carved on it are the words:

In Memory of the Unknown Dead. Who Lost Their Lives in the RAILROAD WRECK of the GREAT WALLACE SHOWS August 6, 1903

Tragedy struck again after the Wallace Circus purchased the Hagenbeck Circus. It was the second largest circus after the Ringling Bros. Circus. On June 22, 1918, in Hammond, Indiana, 86 people died and another 127 were injured when a locomotive engineer fell asleep and ran his troop train into the rear of the circus train.

# Lincoln Brick Factory Ruins

Location:
13991 Tallman Road
Grand Ledge, MI 48837

The Grand River flows through the town of Grand Ledge and large deposits of clay were found along the banks. The Native Americans in the area used the clay to make pottery. In later years, the area became popular for making bricks. In 1914, after purchasing farmland along the Grand River, the Baker Clay Company built a factory for manufacturing bricks. It was the first company in America that used a continuous kiln, which was more productive and developed in Canada. The kilns were constructed close to each other and used a series of tunnels to provide heat more efficiently than separate kilns.

The Baker Clay Co. started out making glazed clay tiles for farm silos. They switched to bricks after the use of concrete became more popular in the construction of silos. The plant changed its name to the The Grand Ledge Face Brick Company. The company manufactured hundreds of thousands of bricks. At its peak the factory could produce 40,000 bricks in a single day, many of which were used in the construction of buildings throughout the state. Several of the buildings at Michigan State University, including Beaumont Tower, were constructed with Grand Ledge bricks.

In the 1940s, the plant was sold to the Lincoln Brick Factory. The factory closed in 1947 and the property was acquired by Eaton County in 1975. The land is now a county park aptly named Lincoln Brick Park. The remnants of the old factory still stand in this park where you can wander around to explore the ruins.

> **Trip Tip**: Lincoln Brick Park is an Eaton County Park and charges visitors a $5 entrance fee. While you are in the area Fitzgerald Park is an Eaton County Park on the other side of the Grand River and offers a hike along the cliffs.

# Kingston Depot

Location:
5918 State Street (M-46)
Kingston, MI 48741

The small town of Kingston sits along M-46 near the heart, or more like the knuckle of the Thumb. Before the automobile became the preferred mode of transportation it was the railroad that could make or break a town. The town of Kingston quickly grew in popularity when the Pontiac Oxford & Port Austin railroad came through and built a depot in 1883. The PO & PA started in Pontiac and ended in Caseville. It was supposed to end in Port Austin as the name suggested, but because of fires around the Port Austin area and the decline of the town it, was decided to run the rail line to Caseville. In 1909, the rail line became part of the Grand Trunk Railroad, by the 1970s, they had discontinued rail service in the thumb and abandoned the tracks.

The little depot was dismantled and stored in a barn near Cass City. In 1993, A century after it was constructed, it was discovered in the barn. Citizens raised money and had the railroad station reconstructed in Memory Park near downtown Kingston along M-46.

Some sections of the old PO & PA railroad line serve as the Polly Ann Rail Trail that runs through Oakland and Lapeer Counties.

# The Skyman

Location:
4300 Hubbardston Road
Pewamo, MI 48873

In the center of the Lower Peninsula near the Maple River is the East Plains Cemetery. It is a rather lonely cemetery surrounded by farmland between the towns of Pewamo and Hubbardston. Next to a headstone is a small handmade historical marker for "Skyman" Philip Parmelee. He was born in 1887, near the small town of

Hubbardston. At an early age Philip's family moved to Marion, Michigan where he became adept at working on small engines. He made an early automobile, when he added a steam engine to a horse buggy fitted with bicycle wheels. He was raised by his father in St. Johns, after his mother was killed by a runaway horse.

Philip worked at a machine shop in St. Johns and honed his skills building small engines. In 1906, he moved to Flint to work for the Buick Motor Car Company. Rumor has it that he took one of Louis Chevrolet's racing cars that was being repaired on a joy ride to Flushing and back.

In 1910, Parmelee joined the Wright Flying School run by Wilbur and Orville Wright. After training, he joined the Wright Exhibition Team. Because of his blond hair, dashing good looks, and fearless flying abilities, he was given the nickname "Skyman". He is credited with making the first commercial flight with an airplane after he delivered a box of silk from Dayton to Columbus. In 1911, he flew a reconnaissance mission for the U.S. Army at the Texas and Mexico border. Later that year, he was the pilot of a Wright Model B when 54-year-old Grant Morton jumped out with a parachute over Venice Beach, California. This was the earliest known jump of a man from an airplane using a parachute.

Tragically, Pilip's life was cut short in 1912 during an exhibition flight in Yakima Washington when his airplane flipped over in turbulence and crashed. His body was sent back to Michigan and he was laid to rest near the town where he was born. If his life had not been cut short who knows what kind of impact he would have had on aviation.

A Michigan historical marker telling the stories of Parmelee's aviation exploits stands by the entrance to the Capital Region International Airport near Lansing.

# Factory One

Location:
303 West Water Street
Flint, MI 48503

Every business has to start somewhere, including large corporations. Long before Steve Jobs and Steve Wozniak began building personal computers in a garage to form

The Apple Company, a couple of guys from Flint built one of the largest automobile companies in the world.

In 1886, William Crapo "Billy" Durant and business partner Josiah Dallas Dort leased a former cotton mill building along the Flint River for twenty five dollars a month. Together they formed the Flint Road Cart Company which eventually became the Durant-Dort Carriage Factory, one of the largest carriage builders in the world, earning the two men millions of dollars in profits.

In the early 1900s, Durant would take control of the Buick Motor Co. and started the acquisition of other automobile manufacturers to form General Motors. Carriage manufacturing ended in 1917, after the automobile replaced the horse and buggy. Josiah Dort then used the building to manufacture automobiles for his newly formed Dort Motor Company, but the short lived company stopped producing cars in 1924.

For the next few decades, the building was used as a warehouse and office space. In the 1980s, it was used for retail space, but the old factory had been slowly deteriorating with age and in need of renovation. In 2013, General Motors purchased the building known as Factory One and restored and preserved it. The historic building is now used as a meeting facility and a community space for events.

Factory One is also home to Kettering University's automotive archive established by Kettering professor Richard P. Scharchburg in 1974. The archives contain about 100,000 documents, photographs, and other artifacts that document Flint's early automotive history.

# Captain Walker's Branded Hand

Location:
391 Irwin Avenue
Muskegon, MI 49442

Near the entrance of Muskegon's historic Evergreen Cemetery, is a tall slender stone monument. Carved into it are the words **Captain Walker's Branded Hand**, along with a carving of a hand with the letters SS on the palm. It is a rather curious stone obelisk and begs the questions,

Who was Captain Walker and why was his hand branded with the letters SS?

In 1799, Jonathan Walker was born in Harwich, Massachusetts where he learned to sail fishing vessels. By the 1830s, he had moved to Florida and sailed ships as a railroad contractor. A known abolitionist and disgusted with slavery in the south, he aided several escaping slaves by sailing them to the British West Indies where slavery had been abolished. On one of these voyages, Captain Walker became gravely ill. His inexperienced crew allowed the ship to be captured by a search boat. Captain walker was arrested and taken to prison where he was chained to the floor in a small dark room for months. After his trial and conviction, he was sentenced to be publicly branded and thrown back in prison. The letters SS were branded into his right hand which indicated he was a slave stealer.

He was released from prison after five years, when northern abolitionists paid for his freedom. He spend the remainder of his life touring the northern states, giving lectures on the evils of slavery and proudly showing people his branded hand. Eventually, he moved to the Muskegon area where he died in 1878. Captain Walker was laid to rest in Evergreen Cemetery and the monument that was erected in his memory still stands near the entrance, proudly showing visitors a reminder of his branded hand.

Several other prominent citizens of Muskegon are laid to rest at Evergreen Cemetery including Charles Hackley and Thomas Hume. Their opulent Victorian mansions stand together at 484 W. Webster Ave.

# Michigan Relics Hoax

Location:
Michigan History Center
702 W. Kalamazoo Street
Lansing, MI 48915

In 1890, James O. Scotford, a sign painter living in the central Michigan town of Edmore, claimed to have found a strange clay cup and carved tablets in the ground near his home. He found more ancient artifacts drawing the attention of investors who would purchase the strange objects with the intention of making a profit by displaying them to the public.

In 1907, Scotford partnered with Daniel E. Soper, former Michigan Secretary of State who had resigned from his position in disgrace after being accused of embezzlement. Scotford would find the artifacts and Soper would sell them. They found thousands of ancient relics in seventeen counties around Michigan. Scotford would take investors out and dig around, looking for relics. When one was found, he would let his investors or landowners remove them from the soil. Nobody knew for sure, but it is believed Scotford used sleight of hand tricks to partially bury the artifacts. Many of the artifacts were slate or copper plates with symbols that looked like ancient writing. No one has been able to decipher the unique hieroglyphics. Some of the plates also have biblical looking drawings such as an ark like Noah's Ark.

When scholars and experts began to look at the artifacts closer, they seemed to be fake. A single artifact would have multiple languages carved into it, and the slate artifacts had modern saw marks. The number of relics found was also suspect. Scotford and Soper "found" artifacts, thousands of artifacts, for almost three decades. The two men never admitted to faking any of the artifacts, and maintained they were authentic to the day of their deaths in the 1920s.

Many of the relics were purchased by The Church of Jesus Christ of Latter-day Saints in the early 1900s, because of their religious theme. As time went on, many experts proved that the artifacts were indeed fakes. By 1960, technology could prove the copper plates were manufactured using modern 20th-century techniques and the plates were not thousands of years old.

The church gave most of the relics to the Michigan History Museum where they were put on display in 2003. Since then, they have been put into storage like the ark in Raiders of the Lost Ark. It has been said to be one of the largest hoaxes in the archaeological world and has brought artifacts found in Michigan into question, with people left wondering if they are legitimate or fake.

The documentary, *Hoax or History: The Michigan Relics* tells the story of Scotford and Soper and their deceit.

# Lake Odessa Train Depot

Location:
1117 Emerson Street
Lake Odessa, MI 48849

The town of Lake Odessa came about from the town of Bonanza which was started in 1887 a few miles to the north. Humphrey R. Wager, from nearby Ionia, purchased about eighty acres and started the town of Bonanza. A year later, after the railroad tracks were laid to the south, the townsfolk decided to move the town closer to the tracks. They moved their houses, businesses, belongings and inventory to the new town site. The new town was given the name Lake Odessa, named after the prominent city in Russia.

A train station was built by the Detroit, Lansing, and Northern Railroad. It is the only Russian Ornate-style depot in the state of Michigan. I can only assume that it was decided to style the depot after the heritage of the town's namesake. The depot welcomed passengers for decades until it closed in 1971. In the 1980s, the building was sold to the historical society and moved to a park at the north end of town where it serves as a historical museum.

Michi-fact: During WWII, Lake Odessa had a Prisoner Of War camp that held German soldiers who worked in the nearby fields.

# Hardy Dam

Location:
36th Street
Newaygo, MI 49337

The Muskegon River flows through the central part of the Lower Peninsula and empties into Lake Michigan in the town of Muskegon. Northeast of Newaygo, three dams were constructed by Consumers Power to generate electricity. The largest of them is the Hardy Dam, constructed in 1929. It was the largest earthen dam in North America, east of the Mississippi River, at the time of its construction. It was named for George Hardy, a partner in the firm that financed Consumers' projects from 1911 through 1928. The dam generates 30,000 kilowatts of electricity which is enough to serve a community of nearly 23,000 people.

A road passes over the top of the dam, similar to the Hoover Dam between Nevada and Arizona. I have never driven over the Hoover Dam, but traversing the road on the Hardy Dam is quite an experience. The road is rather narrow with a concrete wall on one side and a guardrail and drop off on the other.

**Trip Tip**: A park near the dam, on the east side of the river, has some parts of the dam on display and provides some history of it.

# Charlton Park

Location:
2545 S Charlton Park Rd.
Hastings, MI 49058

Southeast of Hastings, along the Thornapple River is a small village that seems to be stuck in time. A church, blacksmith shop, barber shop, general store, and several other buildings that look like they belong in the late 1800s.

Although they were built in the 1800s, they did not originally stand where they do today.

In 1936, Irving Charlton donated property to Barry County for a park. Over the years, several historic buildings from around Barry County were moved to the park. Today they create a historic village which includes the two-story brick building that served as the offices for the Hastings Mutual Insurance Co from 1908 to 1924. Visitors can explore the historic buildings along with a museum that displays artifacts collected by Irving Charlton. During the summer months, the park hosts several events such as, car shows, tractor shows and Civil War reenactments. You can learn more at their website www.Charltonpark.org

Charlton Park is also the location of a settlement known as Indian Landing. In the early 1800s, the Thornapple band of Ottawa Indians established a village a short distance from the Thornapple River. In 1848, four Indian families purchased land here, and remained until their removal to northern Michigan about 1855.

# Sage Library

Location:
100 E. Midland Street
Bay City, MI 48706

The oldest continuously operating library building in Michigan sits in Bay City. Lumberman Henry W. Sage donated land and fifty thousand dollars to construct a building for the citizens of Wenona. That was the name of the village at the time before it became part of Bay City. When the building opened in 1884, the first floor was used as a high school, the second floor was a library, and the third floor was offices for the superintendent of the school. A new school was built nearby and the library's expansive collection of books was able to utilize the entire building. The most important book in the collection is a 1492 Koberger Bible that was gifted to the library in 1900. It is kept safe in a custom made two thousand pound vault.

Along with books, the library is rumored to be home to a few paranormal spirits. There have been some strange occurrences over the years. Librarians have sometimes heard loud heavy footsteps behind them as they work. After turning around, no one is there. When closing up at night, all of the books are neatly organized and sometimes in the morning a few books are found strewn about as if a storm or something, or someone, has moved them in a disorderly manner. Most disturbing is that people have seen a little girl in a white dress on the third floor. Legend has it that she died over a century ago by contracting smallpox from a book she had borrowed from the library.

A fountain and statue "Leda and the Swan" from mythology stands in front of the library. When it was placed at the site decades ago, people were concerned about the semi-nude statue and the fact that it faced the church across the street.

# Hidden Castle

Location:
Pere Marquette Drive
Canadian Lakes, MI 49346

Hidden away in a private community known as Canadian
Lakes is a marvelous concrete castle. In 1974, developer
Donald Bollman purchased swampy farmland between

Mount Pleasant and Big Rapids. He converted the area into a private community with lakes, golf courses and tennis courts for the residents and their guests to enjoy. He built this castle on one of three golf courses in the community. The lower floor served as a banquet center and the upper floor was used as a residence for the Bollman family. After Donald died, the family sold the castle to the Canadian Lakes Property Owners Corp. The castle is known as the Highland Castle named for the golf course adjacent to it. The castle is used for weddings and private functions for residents of the community.

During the Christmas season, the castle is decorated with holiday lights. Visitors can obtain passes on the weekends to see the illuminated castle.

# A Woman's Courage

Location:
900 Saginaw Street
Flint, MI 48502

Next to the Genesee County courthouse in Flint is an ordinary looking Michigan historical marker. It has two names on it. One side with a woman's name and the other side with a man's name. It is a reminder of a remarkable person who lived in Flint over a century ago.

Sarah Emma Edmonds was born in Canada in 1841. To escape her abusive father she dressed as a man and immigrated to Flint in 1857. During the Civil War, on May 25, 1861, she enlisted as Franklin Thompson in Company F of the 2nd Michigan Infantry, also known as the Flint Union Greys. Extensive physical examinations were not required for enlistment and her true identity was not discovered. She served as a nurse and messenger and participated in several battles. She also dressed as a woman and became a spy for the Union. In 1893, Emma (or Frank) became ill and she deserted the army before she was found out to be a woman.

In 1864, Sarah wrote a book about her experiences in the Civil War titled *The Female Spy of the Union Army*. One year later, her story was picked up by a Hartford, CT publisher who issued it with a new title, *Nurse and Spy in the Union Army*. It was a huge success, selling in excess of 175,000 copies. Edmonds donated the profits from her memoir to various soldiers aid organizations. She continued to travel the country lecturing and sharing her remarkable story.

In 1867, she married Linus. H. Seelye, a mechanic and a childhood friend with whom she had three children. All three of their children died in their youth, leading the couple to adopt two sons. She petitioned the government to change her desertion charge and on July 3, 1886, Congress granted Sarah Emma Edmonds Seelye an honorable discharge from combat duty and a pension of $12 a month. She is the only female to be admitted into the veteran's organization the Grand Army of the Republic and is laid to rest in a G.A.R. section of Washington Cemetery in Houston, Texas after she died in 1897

# Chapter 3
# Northern Lower Peninsula

# The Concrete Depot

Location:
5300 Linden Street
Millersburg, MI 49759

The small town of Millersburg is located between Alpena and Cheboygan and was a stop on the Detroit and Mackinac Railway. The town was founded in 1897 by Adrian lumberman C.R. Miller and given the name of Millersburg.

The current Millersburg train depot looks a little different than other depots in Michigan. While most are made using lumber or bricks this one is made with concrete blocks. The town unfortunately suffered from three major fires. In 1908, the Metz fire swept through the area and although it spared the town it did burn a lot of timber in the region. In 1911, a fire in the summer burned over thirty homes and destroyed half of downtown Millersburg.

In 1929, another fire destroyed the east side of downtown including seven buildings and three homes. The original depot built in 1898, burned down in 1914. This concrete depot was constructed in 1917 and has stood for more than a century. I am sure the builders decided to use materials that would minimize the chance of the new depot catching on fire. The railroad abandoned the depot in the 1980s, and it is now used as a museum by the historical society.

The old D&M Railroad tracks are now part of the North Eastern State Trail, used by snowmobilers, cyclists, and hikers. A nice park and picnic area are located next to the historic depot with heated bathroom facilities that are maintained year round.

# Pioneer House

Location:
9991 Marilla Road
Copemish, MI 49625

The small town of Marilla is located between Mesick and
Kaleva at the northern end of the Manistee National
Forest. Marilla  was organized in 1869 and was named

74

after the sister of one of the original members of the township board of supervisors. The largest building in town is an old brick school. It was constructed in 1920 and closed in 1948. By the 1990s, the old school building's upper floor had been converted into township offices and a community center. The lower floor was converted into a museum by the Marilla Historical Society.

Some of the township's historic buildings have been relocated to stand behind the old school. One of the buildings is a hand hewn log home now called "The Pioneer House." It was built in the 1870s, by Aaron Pepple on land that he homesteaded. In 1881, President Garfield signed a grant officially giving the land to the Pepple family. In the early years, before the railroad came through the area, the home was a stopover for the stagecoach and travelers looking for a break. They could get a warm meal and even stay the night to get some rest. I guess you could say it was an early Airbnb long before the internet was even a thing.

There is also a log cabin and a historic early 1900s barn for visitors to see and explore. The cabin was home to Swedish born Nels Johnson who emigrated to the area to work as a lumberjack. The John Sturdevant barn is a mortise and tenon barn that stood southwest of Marilla. The barn is held together with wooden pegs and holds a display of historic agricultural machinery.

**Trip Tip:** The Little Mac Foot Bridge, part of the North Country Trail, is about five miles east of Marilla.

# Irontone Springs

Location:
3600 Old 27 North
Gaylord, MI 49735

For the trolls living in the southern part of the state, I-75 is a quick way to get to the Mackinac Bridge, if it is not stop and go traffic clogged by congestion. Before the interstate was constructed Old 27 was the main route going north and south through the Lower Peninsula. On this early route north Gaylord, is a beautiful roadside park for motorists to stop for a break.

The park is the Frank Wilkinson Park, named in honor of the man who was the first Otsego County road commissioner. He owned the property and deeded it to the county after his death.

The park is also known as Irontone Springs for the iron rich artisan spring that flows all year long. The spring flows into Mossback Creek which flows through the park. A wooden bridge crosses the creek and a trail leads to a pavilion with picnic tables. It is a quiet serene place for travels to stop at for a picnic. If you enjoy chasing waterfalls, large stones in the creek have made some small but pretty falls.

# North Unity

Location:
1035 W. Harbor Hwy (M-22)
Maple City, MI 49664

Along M-22 between Glen Arbor and Leland is an old log cabin. It has ties to the doomed community of North Unity that was located a few miles away near Lake Michigan.

In the 1850s, due to the lack of work in Chicago, some Bohemian (present-day Czech Republic) and German immigrants left the city and sailed Lake Michigan looking for paradise. The men landed in Good Harbor in the Leelanau Peninsula and found a beautiful piece of land to establish a new community which they called North Unity. Typhoid fever was spreading throughout Chicago, so the family and friends of the men of North Unity left in October to join them in the new town. Since winter was coming quickly, they decided to build a large 150-foot long barrack. The inside was divided by walls in order to house each family. They would build houses and establish farms in the spring.

The first winter was extremely challenging for the group. They had brought only a few supplies with them, and because they had arrived at the end of summer, they were not able to grow food to feed their families. The local ponds and lakes were frozen over so they could not fish either. They purchased corn from the local Indians and managed to keep from starving to death until the spring thaw.

In the spring, they built permanent houses and farms. Over the next few years, the little community began to prosper. Other people began moving to the little town in the Leelanau Peninsula. Eventually, a schoolhouse and a gristmill were constructed and John Shalda built a general store. Sadly, forest fires swept through Michigan in 1871 and destroyed most of the buildings and houses of North Unity.

The people of the devastated community moved further inland to the area near the corner of M-22 and Bohemian Road (County Road 669). They started a new community and built new houses and other buildings including a church. John Shalda built a new general store and a log cabin. Not far away a new school was constructed. Most of the buildings are now gone and nothing remains of the original site of North Unity. The log cabin that John Shalda constructed is the one that still stands along M-22.

A few miles to the west is the old schoolhouse for North Unity. It is hidden in the trees but can be seen from the bicycle path.

# Herron Explosion

Location:
3400 Herron Road
Herron, MI 49744

About ten miles southwest of Alpena, among the farm land and forests is the old town of Herron. It was founded by Fred Herron in 1920 and given a post office named after him. The small town never grew in population to be a prominent city but it does have a few

82

houses along with a beautiful little country church. There are a couple of old buildings, one that looks like the remains of an old general store that faded away when it became easier to drive to Alpena to save a few bucks by shopping at the big box superstore.

Most people have never heard of the town of Herron, but half a century ago the little town made national news after a devastating tragedy. On October 30th, 1952, five men were killed when a mine near the town exploded. Six men were searching a nearby long-abandoned gold mine for uranium. According to the only survivor, John Pastuszka, two of the men went down the 180-foot deep shaft to check on water pumps being used to drain it. The other three men were standing around the opening to the shaft when it suddenly exploded. The blast threw the men about three hundred feet along with steel that was covering the hole. Pastuszka was spared because he was standing next to a tool shed when the explosion occurred. It is believed that methane gas and a spark from a drill caused the violent blast.

The gold mine was dug in the early 1900s and it was used as part of a scam to swindle investors. It seems as if that old mine has brought nothing but bad luck and misfortune.

# Elberta Life Saving Station

Location:
1120 Furnace Street
Elberta, MI 49628

84

The town of Elberta is along M-22 on Betsie Lake. This building was built in 1887, and stands across from Frankfort where the Betsie Lake connects to Lake Michigan. It was built as a station for the U.S. Life Saving Service. One man would be in the cupola while another walked the beach watching for ships or sailors in distress. The building was used until 1935 when a new Coast Guard station was built on the other side of the lake in Frankfort. The building was then used by the railroad for offices and as a marine center. It is now part of Elberta's Waterfront Park and used as a hall for wedding receptions and parties.

I can't imagine how challenging it would have been to work in the U.S. Life Saving Service. Rowing out into a winter storm on a raging Lake Michigan must have been truly terrifying and physically draining. The unofficial motto of the Life Service is. "You have to go out, but you don't have to come back."

The ruins of the Frankfort Iron Works also stand in the park near the old life saving station.

# Big Rock Nuke Plant

Location:
9550 US-31
Charlevoix, MI 49720

North of Charlevoix, along US-31, is a scenic roadside park that overlooks Lake Michigan. It is the location of a historical marker that recalls a time when a nuclear power plant stood not far from the little park.

In the summer of 1960, construction began on Michigan's first nuclear power plant. It was the fifth nuclear plant in the United States and was named after its location on Big Rock Point. The plant began as a research and development facility, with the goal of being able to prove that nuclear power was a viable means of generating electricity. It was the world's first high-power density boiling water reactor and built by General Electric. The plant also produced cobalt 60 used in radio therapy to eradicate cancer. It is estimated that while the plant operated, it produced enough cobalt 60 to treat 400,000 cancer patients.

After the completion of the power plant, the United States Air Force Strategic Air Command used the plant to train bomber pilots. B52 bombers would fly over the plant on simulated training missions. On January 7, 1971, a low flying B52 crashed into Lake Michigan, killing all nine crew members. It was a tragic day but would have been incomprehensible if the plane had crashed a few seconds later into the nuclear power plant. When the public learned more about the training missions and became aware of how close Michigan came to a nuclear disaster, the flight paths were changed in order to avoid the plant.

The Big Rock Point plant closed in 1997 and was dismantled. During the decommissioning process, it was discovered that a backup safety system at the plant had been inoperable for at least fourteen years. In the event of a control rod failure, the system should have drained a boron solution into the core, halting the nuclear chain reaction. However, during decommissioning when technicians attempted to drain the tank, they were unable to do so due to a corroded pipe. If something would have gone wrong at the plant, the system used to contain it would in all likelihood failed.

After all the buildings and structures were removed, the land was converted back to the way it was before the construction. There were plans to convert the property into a park, but it remains closed and gated off to the public.

When the nuclear plant was first being built, General Electric ran promotional videos hosted by future president Ronald Reagan, who was a spokesman for GE at the time.

# Daughters Of The American Revolution Forest

Location:
Old US Hwy 27
Houghton Lake, MI 48629
44.226779, -84.792030

Between Clare and Houghton Lake, along old US-27, is a large stone marker. On it is carved:

**Forest of Louisa St. Clair Chapter Daughters of the American Revolution Detroit Mich. A.D. 1929.**

One of the earliest chapters of the Daughters Of The American Revolution was formed in Detroit in 1893. The chapter was named for Louisa St. Clair, the daughter of General Arthur St. Clair, Governor of the Northwest Territory. It was one of the fastest growing chapters in the country and by the 1920s, it had over six hundred members.

In 1928, The Louisa St. Clair chapter of the D.A.R. purchased seedlings and over the next two years, they oversaw trees planted on two hundred acres of clear-cut forests. They embedded pine trees among the stumps to regrow the barren land in the forests north of Clare. It was the first D.A.R. forest in the nation and other chapters followed suit, planting forests in their states. Upon completion of their project, they erected the stone monument which still stands to this day. The next time you are driving north of Clare, I hope you will remember the women from Detroit that planted the trees for future generations to enjoy.

In 2015, for the 85th anniversary of the placing of the monument the current members of the Louisa St. Clair chapter of the D.A.R. rededicated the stone monument.

# Nature Megaphone

Location:
4507 Big Sky Trail
Indian River, MI 49749
45.394818, -84.535269

The Pigeon River winds its way through the northern part of the Lower Peninsula and flows into Mullet Lake. The Agnes S. Andreae Nature Preserve and adjoining Boyd B. Banwell Family Nature Preserve contain 181 acres of wilderness along the Pigeon River near Afton.

In 1983, Agnes S. Andreae donated twenty seven acres along with her cabin, named "Pigeon Cote", to the Little Traverse Bay Land Conservancy. The cabin was built in 1908 and was purchased by Agnes' mother in 1920. The family enjoyed it for decades before Agnes kindly donated it for public use. A splendid wooden footbridge was constructed over the Pigeon River near the cabin. It is not the longest footbridge in the state, but it is impressive in size and provides a breathtaking view as you cross over it.

Deep within the preserve is a large tubular structure that sits on a hill overlooking a valley near the Pigeon River. If you sit inside it, you will hear the surrounding sounds of nature. Dubbed the Nature Megaphone, it was constructed in 2019 by students of Petoskey High

School's Building Trades with lumber donated by the Petoskey Home Depot. The megaphone is located about two miles away from Agnes's old cabin. It is not the easiest of hikes, and it was a little muddy when I vistited, but it is worth the trip.

If you want to visit the cabin and megaphone, the official parking area for the Agnes S. Andreae Nature Preserve is at the intersection of Riverwoods Trail and Big Sky Trail roads east of Indian River. The parking area for Boyd B. Banwell Family Nature Preserve is off M-68 about one hundred yards east of where it crosses the Pigeon River.

The land conservancy rents out the cabin to scouting troops and non-profit community groups.

# White Shoal Lighthouse

## Location:
## Northern Lake Michigan

Guiding ships into the western end of the Straits of Mackinac is the White Shoal Lighthouse. It sits miles away from land in northern Lake Michigan. The light was a marvel of engineering when it was constructed in 1908 and completed in 1910. It has a unique "candy cane" red and white stripe paint scheme and is the only lighthouse on the Great Lakes with a helical style design.

The tower is 121 feet tall, making it the tallest lighthouse on the Great Lakes. It has living quarters inside for the keepers who maintain the beacon. It was one of a handful of lighthouses on the Great Lakes to have a second order Fresnel lens. When the light was automated in 1975, the lens was removed and put on display at the Whitefish Point Shipwreck Museum. Another unique feature is that it has an aluminum lantern room instead of cast iron. Because of its aesthetics, an image of the White Shoal

Lighthouse was used by State of Michigan for the "Save our Lights" license plates fundraising campaign.

White Shoal Light Historical Preservation Society is a non-profit group that is in the process of restoring the lighthouse to the way it would have been in the 1950s. They have plans to open it up to visitors for tours and overnight stays. You can find more information at their website www.preservewhiteshoal.org.

One way to see the historic lighthouse is to take a Shepler's Lighthouse Cruise. Passengers board in order of ticket sales.

# Rockport State Park

Location:
Old Grade Road
Alpena, MI 49707

Rockport State Recreation Area is one of Michigan's newest and most unique state parks. Many of northern Michigan state parks are known for their campgrounds, sandy beaches and wooded hiking trails. Rockport however, has an old stone quarry, sink holes and a rocky shoreline for rock hunters to search for their favorite stone.

From 1914 until the end of the 1950s, the site operated as a stone quarry, loading freighters in a deep harbor with large mechanical loading dock. The final shipments of stone were for the foundations of the Mackinac Bridge. After that, the quarry closed and the buildings, along with the homes for the workers, were removed. The foundations of the loading dock still stretches out into the crystal clear blue water of Lake Huron.

The land was given to Consumers Power after the quarry departed the site. In the 1990s, the property was given to the DNR to manage. In 2012 the once abandoned quarry officially became the states 100th state park. Visitors have the opportunity to hike and explore the rocky landscape, where remnants of structures and machinery from the old quarry can be found along the trails. Visitors can also make the two mile hike to see some of the parks several sink holes. During the night time, the stars and Milky Way can be clearly seen since the park is one of the states official dark sky parks. Rock hounds are welcomed to look for Petoskey stones and fossils and although it is illegal to remove rocks from most state and federal land, Rockport State Recreation Area allows visitors to remove up to twenty-five pounds of rocks per person per year. If you are looking for something different to do or see be sure to visit Rockport S.R.A., north of Alpena, on the sunrise side of the state.

The ghost town of Bell (featured in volume 3 of *Lost in Michigan*) can be found about five miles to the north in the Besser Natural Area.

# St Francis Solanus Indian Mission

Location:
430 W. Lake Street
Petoskey, MI 49770

West of   downtown Petoskey overlooking Little Grand
Traverse Bay is a small brown church. It is surrounded by
a white picket fence and wooden crosses.

Jean Baptiste Trotochaud and his Ojibwa wife Sophia Anaquet purchased land from an Odawa Indian named Amawee. Trotochaud donated nearly an acre of land to the Catholic Church. The mission was built in 1859 and blessed by Bishop Frederic Baraga.

Natives and settlers used the simple wooden church for services until it was abandoned in the 1890s. It was restored in 2008 and tours of the historic church are given on Sundays in the summer months.

It is the oldest building still standing in Petoskey, and one of the oldest structures in northern lower Michigan.

# Chapter Four
# Upper Peninsula

# Highest Natural Point In Michigan

Location:
Huron Mountains
46.755874900606436,
-88.15534549087167

The highest natural point in Michigan is at the summit of
Mount Arvon in the Huron Mountain Range which lies
between Marquette and L'Anse. Mt. Arvon's peak is 1979

feet above sea level. A sign marks the highest point at the top, along with a U.S. Geological Survey benchmark (round metal marker) and a mailbox with a logbook.

If you are physically fit and adventurous, there is a two-mile hiking trail that leads to the summit. If the thought of hiking two miles uphill sounds like torture, you can drive right up to it. Mt. Arvon is about a thirty mile trek from L'Anse. The last fifteen miles are up winding gravel forest roads that makes the destination a real accomplishment to visit. You could probably drive to it in a passenger car, but I would recommend an SUV or truck. It would be best to make the journey in the summer months, avoiding early spring when there is still snow on the roads in the Huron Mountains. The snow also makes the roads muddy and impassible at times. If you take the trip, be sure to stop at the Baraga Convention and Vistor's Bureau center in L'Anse for directions and info on road conditions.

If you are looking for a place in Michigan to add to your bucket list, this is a good one. Just be sure to plan on a couple of hours driving there and back from L'Anse. One last thing, do not rely on your GPS to take you there. You want to get to Mt. Arvon by driving south on Roland Lake Road from Skanee Road. Follow the light blue diamond signs that direct motorists to the summit.

For decades, the nearby summit of Mt. Curwood was believed to be the tallest point in Michigan. During a survey in the 1980s, it was determined that Mt. Arvon is eleven inches taller.

# Christmas Lighthouse

Location:
M-28 West of Munising
46.4369910411884,
-86.69133152738276

West of Munising along Lake Superior and M-28 is the town of Christmas. Gamblers know of the town for the large "log cabin" style casino that welcomes people wanting to try their luck. Tourist to the Upper Peninsula know about the little town because of its unique name. The town got its name in 1938, when Julius Thorton built a factory to make holiday gifts. I am confused as to whether he named the town or his factory Christmas. Unfortunately, in the summer of 1940, the business burned down and was never rebuilt. The workshop no longer exists, but the area still kept the name Christmas.

After the Civil War, as shipping increased on Lake Superior, many vessels sailed between Grand Island and the mainland to seek refuge from the numerous storms. A pair of lights, known as range lights, were erected on the shoreline near Christmas to guide sailors into the channel. A small wooden tower was built near the edge of Lake Superior and a lighthouse was constructed further back.

By the early 1900s, the Grand Island Harbor Range lighthouse was in need of repair so the decision was made to replace it and the keeper with an automated system. A conical iron tower was constructed in 1913, with an acetylene light that would automatically ignite when the sun valve opened. When the sun went down the valve would automatically open and the gas eliminated the need for electricity to be ran to the lighthouse.

By the 1960s ships were so large that many could not use the narrow passage around Grand Island for safety. In 1969, the rear light was decommissioned and permanently turned off. It is not an overly impressive lighthouse, but it is one of the tallest iron tower navigational lights on the Great Lakes. It is currently under the ownership and care of the National Forest Service and is part of the Hiawatha National Forest.

If you want to visit the old iron tower, the easiest way to find it is to look for the "Welcome to Christmas" sign east of town. There is a sandy parking area and a trail that leads to the water and front range light. A two track road leads to the old iron tower across the road.

The original wood framed lighthouse was moved to Munising and still stands as a private residence. The tower was removed and only those that know its history are aware that it was once a lighthouse.

# Chippewa County Courthouse

Location:
319 Court Street,
Sault Ste. Marie, MI 49783

Sault Ste. Marie is the oldest city in Michigan so it is no surprise that one of the oldest courthouses in the Great Lakes State can be found there. It stands along Bingham Avenue, named for Reverend Abel Bingham. The

Reverend was sent to Sault Ste. Marie by the American Baptist Missionary Society in the late 1820s to organize a temperance society and school. It was on the lot where the school once stood that the courthouse was constructed in 1877.

The Second Empire building was constructed with limestone from Drummond Island and trimmed in red sandstone extracted from the second canal. The walls of this historic building are two feet thick in some places. An addition was added to the rear of the building in 1904 using the same stone as the original building.

The old courthouse was added to the list of National Historic Places in 1984, and was renovated in 1989. A wooden statue of Lady Justice stands on the clock tower, watching the ships pass through the Soo Locks which are a few blocks away.

The Chippewa County Courthouse is the only courthouse in the state of Michigan that has served its residents continuously since its construction.

# St Anthony's Rock

Location:
Near 55 Central Hill
St Ignace, MI 49781

Saint Ignace is a popular destination for travelers since it is at the northern end of the Mackinac Bridge and is a place where you can take the ferry over to Mackinac Island. The downtown area has many restaurants and gift shops for tourists to explore. Behind the shops, next to the parking lot, is a large rock surrounded by a metal picket fence. It is known as St. Anthony's Rock.

The rock was formed millions of years ago when sea caves collapsed. It is what geologists refer to as a landlocked sea stack or sea chimney. It is similar to several features on Mackinac Island, such as Arch Rock or Sugar Loaf and the nearby Castle Rock, next to I-75.

Legend has it that the rock was named by Father Louis Hennepin while exploring the Great Lakes in 1679 on La Salle's boat the *Griffon*. La Salle believed that St. Anthony of Padua would protect his ship and crew on their exploration of the Great Lakes. During a violent storm on Lake Huron, Fr. Hennepin prayed to St. Anthony for protection. When the ship made it to the safety of the fur trading town of St Ignace, the sailors named the rock in honor of their patron saint.

In the late 1880s, the rock became a popular tourist attraction as the railroad bringing tourists to the area wound its way past the large rock.

# The Stone Ship

Location:
Near 58874 US-41,
Calumet Twp, MI 49913

North of Calumet, US-41 winds through the center of the Keweenaw Peninsula. The road passes by Veterans Memorial Park in the town of Kearsarge. At the center of the park is a large stone ship with a mining drill mounted on the bow to represent a gun. It is difficult to drive past this unique looking ship and not wonder about who built it and why is it located in the Keweenaw.

The *U.S.S. Kearsarge* was built in a Maine shipyard for the Union Navy during the Civil War. At the time of its construction, it was a state of the art warship, named for nearby Mt. Kearsarge. After the war, one of the officers who served on the ship moved to the Keweenaw to work for the Hecla Mining Company. He named the company town Kearsarge in honor of the ship he served on during the war.

By the 1930s, the Great Depression had severely cut copper production and mining in the Upper Peninsula and workers were in desperate need of support. Franklin D. Roosevelt's New Deal provided government sponsored work programs to give people jobs on civilian projects. The WPA (Works Progress Administration) built many of the area's bridges, public buildings, and roads. In 1934, the WPA built the stone ship that sits along the road in Kearsarge. It does not resemble the Civil War ship or any of the other four U.S. Navy ships that were named *Kearsarge*, but the forty foot long stone ship is a nice tribute to these ships and the men and women who served on them.

The WPA built two other stone ships. One of them can be seen in a park in the Centennial Heights neighborhood north of Calumet, on the corner of Jefferson and 1st streets. The other ship was built a few miles north of Hancock, but unfortunately the harsh Michigan weather has reduced it to a pile of stone and rubble.

# The Big Red Lighthouse

Location:
300 N. Lakeshore Blvd.
Marquette, MI 49855

Standing on a rocky shoreline is a large two story red
lighthouse that guides ships into Marquette harbor. It is
one of the oldest structures in the Upper Peninsula's

largest city. It was constructed in 1865 to replace an earlier lighthouse that was constructed in the 1850s. It was one of the first lighthouses built on Lake Superior. The area around Marquette was rich with iron ore deposits which is how it became a prominent city in the U.P.

When the current lighthouse was constructed, it was only one and a half stories tall. In 1910, an assistant keeper was needed to help with the fog signal and breakwater light. A second story was added as living quarters for the assistant keeper. In 1965, the lighthouse was painted red to make it more visible in daytime. The Coast Guard operated the lighthouse as a residence for some of the coasties stationed in Marquette, but the last resident moved out in 1998.

The lighthouse is now owned by the city of Marquette. The nearby Maritime Museum gives tours of the historic lighthouse. On occasion, tour guides and visitors have seen the ghost of a little girl wearing a 1910s style dress. Sometimes she is seen staring out of the window over

Lake Superior or on the catwalk around the lantern. She seems to like showing her spirit to women and other children.

There was no reported death of a little girl at the lighthouse. However, near the turn of the century, a keeper's young daughter was badly injured when she fell on the rocks at the shoreline. I don't know if it is actually haunted, but strangely a lot of keepers have abruptly resigned their duties while serving at the big red lighthouse.

# Fort Wilkins

Location:
15223 US-41,
Copper Harbor, MI 49918

The town of Copper Harbor sits at the tip of the Keweenaw Peninsula. It is the northern end of civilization in Michigan and is rather remote even in modern times. Two centuries ago, it was isolated and nearly inaccessible, but that did not prevent the copper boom. The abundance of copper in the region and the natural harbor gave the town its name. As the population of miners grew, the U.S. government decided that it was necessary to build a military fort to protect the copper mines from the British and to keep the peace with the local Native Americans.

Fort Wilkins was established along the shoreline of Lake Fanny Hooe in 1844 and was named for the Secretary of War William Wilkins. Twenty-seven structures were built including a guardhouse, powder magazine, officer's quarters, two barracks, two mess halls, a hospital, a bakery, and a blacksmith's shop. After two years the fort was deemed unnecessary and the men stationed at it were sent to Texas to fight in the war with Mexico. Sergeant William Wright stayed as a single caretaker of the fort until his death in 1855.

The fort was briefly used after the Civil War because the U.S. Army needed a place for men to serve out the rest of their enlistments. I have a feeling they were not happy about being sent to the tip of the Keweenaw. It must have felt more like a punishment, especially in winter. By 1870 the fort had been completely abandoned by the military. In 1923, the fort and nearby lighthouse became a state park. In 1939, with help from the Work Projects Administration (WPA) the few remaining original buildings were renovated and the rest of the fort was reconstructed. A campground and shower buildings were also created at that time.

Today, Fort Wilkins Historic State Park serves as both a campground and a historic site, welcoming visitors throughout the summer. It is a wonderful place to roam around exploring the buildings to see and feel what it must have been like to live in the remote fort in the mid 1800s.

The flag that flies over the historic fort is a twenty-six star flag. The design would have been the nation's flag in 1844 when the fort was constructed.

# Edge of Michigan

Location:
Parking area off Lake Superior Rd.
46.56493552241006,
-90.41527622679918

While traveling across the Upper Peninsula, I got to wondering how far west I could travel in Michigan. I headed towards Lake Superior from Ironwood and then worked my way south along the shoreline. I got to the Montreal River that forms part of the boundary between Michigan and Wisconsin.

I had to hike down a steep and crudely paved road to reach the westernmost point of Michigan that is at the mouth of the river. I was not greeted by a marker or anything man-made. But, the shoreline was covered with rocks and stones making it a great place for rock hounds to find a natural treasure.

A short hike along the shoreline of the Montreal River took me to an old power plant. I continued past the old structure still in operation and along the reddish brown rocky shoreline. I rounded the corner to get a spectacular view of Superior Falls. The trail along the river came to an end as it became sheer vertical rock cliff that have been eroded away for the past million years. Although an official sign or landmark does not mark the western most point of Michigan. I think the end of the trail looking at the falls is an acceptable location for me to be able to cross it off my bucket list.

If you visit and are not physically able to make the steep trek down to the shoreline, you can head south from the parking area, through the trees to get a good view overlooking Superior Falls.

# Nonesuch Mine

Location:
Porcupine Mountains Wilderness
State Park
Parking area off South Boundry Rd.
46.75825922888619,
-89.61962943155588

The Porcupine Mountains in the western Upper Peninsula is the largest state park in Michigan. It's known for hiking trails, waterfalls, and the Lake Of The Clouds. Few people know that hidden among the trees are the ruins of an old mining town. The town of Nonesuch was created when mining near the Little Iron River began in 1867. The town and mine were named for nonesuch, a type of copper ore that exists in sandstone.

At its peak, the town had a population of 300 people. Along with the mining buildings, the small town had a school, boarding houses, stables, and even a baseball team. Extracting the fine copper particles out of the sandstone was a labor intensive process and by 1912 the mine had closed.

Stone walls and cast iron machine parts from the mine can still be found in the area where the town once stood. The best way to get to the ruins is to take South Boundary Road east from the visitors center. Where the road curves south you will find a dirt road that leads to a parking area with some signage for the old mine. A footpath about a half-mile long leads to the historic mine site.

Near the mine ruins are the Nonesuch Falls on the Little Iron River. They are not overly impressive waterfalls but they are an added bonus if you make the hike to see the stone walls.

# Mansfield and the Mine

Location:
300 Stream Rd. north of Alto Rd.
Crystal Falls, MI 49920
46.118624840567854,
-88.22017247548422

This cute little log cabin church sits north of Crystal Falls near the Michigamme River in the heart of the Upper Peninsula. The church was part of Mansfield, a small town that sprang up when ore was discovered in the area and mining began. Built in the late 1800s, it was the only church in Mansfield. It was maintained by a Lutheran Congregation but used by other faiths.

The mine that started the little town but also upended the town because of its tragic end. The mine was dug under the Michigamme River and miners claimed that they could hear the rushing water from the river above them. That did not stop the mine from expanding the shafts to extract ore until one tragic day. On September 28, 1893, the mine collapsed and the water from the river rushed in, drowning twenty seven men. Their bodies were never recovered and have been entombed under the river for eternity.

When mining ended, the town's population dwindled. The church was used as a shingle mill and later fell into ruin. In the 1970s a group of citizens formed a non-profit organization that restored the little church and continues to preserve the history of the area for travelers to visit.

In 1976, a stone memorial listing the names of the men was placed near the river, marking the location of the tragic event.

# Nahma

Location:
The Nahma Historical Museum
8152 Tamarack Street
Nahma, MI 49864

The town of Nahma stands along the Lake Michigan shoreline in Big Bay De Noc east of Escanaba at the mouth of the Sturgeon River. The town got its name from the river and the fish that swam in it because Nahma is a Native American word for sturgeon.

131

The town was established in 1881 by the Bay de Noquet Lumber Company of Oconto, Wisconsin. At its peak, the company employed over 1500 people and built housing and stores for its employees. The company closed in 1951 and put the entire town up for sale making national headlines. The unique opportunity to purchase a whole town was featured in several newspapers and also an article in Life magazine. An Indiana playground manufacturer purchased Nahma with the intentions to convert the town into a resort community but never had the funding to do it. Eventually the houses and buildings were sold off to individuals.

The town survives to this day and welcomes tourists who are enjoying the Upper Peninsula. It is about four miles south of US-2 and is a nice side trip when traveling across the U.P. Tourists can visit the old generals store or get a meal at the Nahma Inn. An old steam locomotive used by the sawmill stands on display in the park near the center of town.

The town was known for a historic wood burner that looked like an old metal silo. Sadly, it collapsed in 2019.

# Bibliography

The Cannon on the Red Arrow Highway

https://k1025.com/red-arrow-highway/
https://pikelife.com/stories/red-arrow-highway/
https://www.roadsideamerica.com/tip/33672
https://en.wikipedia.org/wiki/4.7-inch_gun_M1906


A House And The BB Gun

https://encyclopediaofarkansas.net/entries/daisy-outdoor-products-2735/
https://www.daisy.com/about-us/
https://www2.dnr.state.mi.us/HistoricalMarkers/


The Walker Tavern at Cambridge Junction

https://www.michigan.org/property/cambridge-junction-historic-state-park-walker-tavern-historic-site
https://www.mlive.com/news/jackson/2014/10/peek_through_time_from_gruelin.html
https://en.wikipedia.org/wiki/Walker_Tavern

The Notch of Michigan

https://lib.msu.edu/branches/map/Miboundaries/
https://www.mlive.com/living/jackson/2010/09/tri-border_where_indiana_michi.html
https://www.michigan.gov/dmva/0,9665,7-402-100108_3003_3009-16934--,00.html
http://absolutemichigan.com/michigan/why-we-are-called-the-wolverine-state/

The Keeper at South Haven

http://lakeeffectliving.com/wordpress/lighting-the-lake-south-havens-civil-war-lighthouse-keeper-james-donahue/
https://wmich.edu/library/lighthouse-logs-collection
https://www.michigan.org/article/trip-idea/the-keepers-behind-haunted-lighthouses-michigan

Mail Order Church

https://www.southlyonmi.org/residents/community/witch_s_hat_depot.php
https://www.southlyonmi.org/departments/parks_and_recreation/little_village_chapel.php

The Wing House

https://branchcountyhistoricalsociety.org/wing-house-museum/
https://sah-archipedia.org/buildings/MI-01-BR5
http://www.michmarkers.com/

Meads Mill Ruins

https://northvilletownshiphistoricfund.org/lost-history

https://www.nailhed.com/2014/02/modest-ruins-of-western-wayne-county.html

Slayton Arboretum

https://www.hillsdale.edu/about/facilities/slayton-aboretum/

https://en.wikipedia.org/wiki/Slayton_Arboretum

https://www.michigan.org/property/slayton-arboretum-hillsdale-college

Niles Train Depot

https://www.greatamericanstations.com/stations/niles-mi-nls/

https://maps.roadtrippers.com/us/niles-mi/activities/niles-rail-depot

http://www.michiganrailroads.com/stations-locations/75-berrien-county-11/539-niles-mi

http://dodgemotorcar.com/history/early_history.php

Haven Hill Ford Lodge

https://www.fohravolunteers.org/havenhillhistory

http://www.havenhillproject.org/

https://henryford150.com/haven-hill/

The House of Eights

https://octagonhouse.org/history/

https://en.wikipedia.org/wiki/Loren_Andrus_Octagon_House

https://theclio.com/entry/111683

Circus Train Disaster

https://www.shiawasseehistory.com/circus.html

https://www.atlasobscura.com/places/great-wallace-shows-circus-train-wreck-memorial

https://99wfmk.com/durandcircustrainwreck2018/

Lincoln Brick Factory Ruins

http://travelthemitten.com/family-trips/explore-the-ruins-and-trails-at-lincoln-brick-park-in-eaton-county-photo-gallery/

https://www.eatoncounty.org/DocumentCenter/View/2498/Lincoln-Brick-Map-Brochure-PDF?bidId=

https://grandledgehistory.wordpress.com/2009/09/04/grand-ledge-face-brick-co-1914-1947/

Kingston Depot

https://www.abandonedrails.com/pontiac-oxford-and-port-austin-railroad

http://www.railroadmichigan.com/railroaddepotmuseums.html

The Skyman

https://www.earlyaviators.com/eparmal1.htm

https://ohiohistorycentral.org/w/Phillip_Parmalee

https://www2.dnr.state.mi.us/HistoricalMarkers/

Factory One

https://www.gmfactoryone.com/product/public/us/en/factory-one/home.html
https://www.gm.com/stories/factory-one
https://www.mlive.com/news/flint/2017/05/tour_general_motors_birthplace.htm


Captain Walker's Branded Hand

https://www.masshist.org/database/viewer.php?item_id=154&pid=15
http://www.thegreatlakespilot.com/stories/JonathanWalker.html
https://www.co.muskegon.mi.us/768/Jonathan-Walker


Michigan Relics Hoax

https://archive.archaeology.org/0405/reviews/michigan.html
http://harris23.msu.domains/event/1907-michigan-relics-the-most-colossal-hoax-of-the-century/
https://www.michiganradio.org/investigative/2017-05-24/fake-relics-found-in-michigan-at-turn-of-century-still-provoke-interest
http://michigansotherside.com/the-mysterious-michigan-relics/


Lake Odessa Train Depot

http://www.lakeodessa.org/our-history.html
http://www.michiganrailroads.com/stations-locations/98-ionia-county-34/954-lake-odessa-mi
https://www.fox17online.com/2013/02/26/historical-train-depot-houses-antique-artifacts

## Hardy Dam

http://genealogytrails.com/mich/newaygo/hardy.html

http://travelthemitten.com/landmarks/croton-and-hardy-dams-in-newaygo-county-historic-landmarks-on-the-muskegon-river/

http://industrialscenery.blogspot.com/2018/06/1907-croton-and-1931-hardy-dams-and.html

https://en.wikipedia.org/wiki/Hardy_Dam

## Charlton Park

https://www.charltonpark.org/

https://www.pbs.org/video/destination-michigan-hastings-historic-charlton-park/

https://www.tripadvisor.com/Attraction_Review-g42294-d6922141-Reviews-Historic_Charlton_Park-Hastings_Barry_County_Michigan.html

## Sage Library

http://www.mybaycity.com/scripts/p3_v2/P3V3-0200.cfm?P3_ArticleID=9257

https://www.baycountylibrary.org/about/hours-locations/historical-sage-library

https://www.mlive.com/news/bay-city/2014/01/sage_librarys_130th_birthday_l.html

Beauchamp, Nicole. Haunted Bay City Michigan. Haunted America, a Division of The History Press, 2020.

## Hidden Castle

https://www.facebook.com/castleincanadianlakes/

https://www.onlyinyourstate.com/michigan/little-known-castle-mi/

https://www.evepla.com/US/Canadian-Lakes/148933825563603/The-Castle-in-Canadian-Lakes

A woman's Courage

https://www.battlefields.org/learn/biographies/sarah-emma-edmonds
https://www.nps.gov/people/sarah-emma-edmonds.htm
https://www.britannica.com/biography/Sarah-Edmonds
https://www2.dnr.state.mi.us/HistoricalMarkers/

The Concrete Depot

http://www.michiganrailroads.com/stations-locations/135-presque-isle-county-71/1796-millersburg-mi
http://freepages.rootsweb.com/~dunn/genealogy/Onaway/1911.htm
https://piadvance.com/2010/09/surviving-the-test-of-time-and-fire/
https://content.govdelivery.com/accounts/MIDNR/bulletins/663a7e
Michigan Place Names, Walter Romig, 1986

Pioneer House

https://marillahistory.org/
https://www.visitmanisteecounty.com/web-2-0-directory/marilla-museum-and-pioneer-place
https://99wfmk.com/marilla-michigan/

Irontone Springs

https://www.gaylordmichigan.net/see-go-irontone-springs-hot-spot-cool-drink/
https://www.otsegocountymi.gov/Facilities/Facility/Details/Irontone-Springs-2
http://otsegocountyparksrec.com/web/wb/pages/irontone-springs.php

North Unity

https://www.nps.gov/slbe/learn/historyculture/northunity.htm
https://leelanau.com/north-unity-michigan/
https://glenarborsun.com/north-unity-a-bohemian-ghost-town/


Herron Explosion

https://usminedisasters.miningquiz.com/saxsewell/herron.htm
http://www.us-data.org/mi/alpena/disaster/mine-explosion-1952.txt
Michigan Place Names, Walter Romig, 1986


Elberta Life Saving Station

https://www.atlanticarea.uscg.mil/Our-Organization/District-9/Ninth-District-Units/Sector-Lake-Michigan/Units/Frankfort/History/
http://villageofelberta.com/wp-content/uploads/2012/03/history.jpg


Big Rock Nuke Plant

https://www.nrc.gov/info-finder/decommissioning/power-reactor/big-rock-point.html
https://www.hmdb.org/m.asp?m=97483
https://ss.sites.mtu.edu/mhugl/2017/11/15/michigans-nearly-endured-nuclear-disaster/

Daughters of the American Revolution Forestt

https://www.louisastclairchapter.org/our-mission/
https://www.louisastclairchapter.org/chapter-history/
https://www.houghtonlakeresorter.com/articles/monument-to-conservation-rededicated/

Nature Megaphone

https://landtrust.org/boyd-b-banwell-nature-preserve/
https://www.detroitnews.com/story/news/local/michigan/2019/07/26/natures-megaphone-helps-bring-northern-michigan-woods-alive/1831798001/
https://landtrust.org/agnes-s-andreae-nature-preserve/

Rockport State Park

https://grkids.com/rockport-state-recreation-area/
http://www.us23heritageroute.org/location.asp?ait=av&aid=346
https://www.freep.com/story/travel/2016/08/06/michigans-strangest-park-rockport/87260930/

White Shoal Lighthouse

https://www.preservewhiteshoal.org/
www.lighthousefriends.com/light.asp?ID=210
https://lightlistening.org/keepers-of-historic-events/

St. Francis Solanus Indian Mission

https://www.michigan.org/property/st-francis-solanus-indian-mission-church
https://petoskeyarea.com/places/st-francis-solanus-indian-mission-church/
https://www2.dnr.state.mi.us/HistoricalMarkers/

Highest Natural Point In Michigan

https://www.baragacounty.org/convention-visitors-bureau/things-to-do/mt-arvon/
https://www.summitpost.org/mount-arvon/151786
https://www.alltrails.com/trail/us/michigan/mount-arvon-michigan-highpoint

Christmas Lighthouse

https://www.fs.usda.gov/recarea/hiawatha/recarea/?recid=18198
Michigan Place Names, Walter Romig, 1986
https://www.lighthousefriends.com/light.asp?ID=570
http://www.terrypepper.com/lights/superior/grandrange/index.html

Chippewa County Courthouse

http://www.courthouses.co/us-states/m/michigan/chippewa-county/
https://www.saultstemarie.com/soo-area-and-great-waters-region/historical-downtown-buildings/
https://www.midwestguest.com/2015/02/court-still-in-session-in-michigans-historic-chippewa-county-courthouse.html

St Anthony's Rock

http://travelthemitten.com/landmarks/michigan-roadside-attractions-st-anthonys-rock-st-ignace/

https://www.saintignace.org/history-of-st-ignace/tidbits-of-history/

https://en.wikipedia.org/wiki/St._Anthony%27s_Rock

The Stone Ship

https://www.roadsideamerica.com/tip/26016

https://ss.sites.mtu.edu/mhugl/2019/10/25/uss-kearsarge-monument/

The Big Red Lighthouse

https://mqtmaritimemuseum.com/marquette-lighthouse/

https://www.lighthousefriends.com/light.asp?ID=572

https://abc10up.com/2014/06/13/ghost-haunts-marquette-harbor-lighthouse/

Fort Wilkins

https://www.exploringthenorth.com/wilkins/wilkins.html

http://www.fortwilkinsnha.org/history.html

https://en.wikipedia.org/wiki/Fort_Wilkins_Historic_State_Park

Edge of Michigan

https://www.world-of-waterfalls.com/waterfalls/eastern-us-superior-falls/

https://gowaterfalling.com/waterfalls/superior.shtml

https://northwoodswisconsin.com/northern-wisconsin-recreation/superior-falls/

Nonesuch Mine

https://www.ghosttowns.com/states/mi/nonesuch.html

https://www.uptravel.com/listing/nonesuch-mine-porcupine-mountains-state-park/2917/

Michigan Ghost Towns of the Upper Peninsula, R.L.Dodge, Thunder bay Press, 1973

Nahma

Company Towns Of Michigan's Upper Peninsula, Christian Holmes, The History Press, 2015

https://www.visitescanaba.com/about/community/nahma/

https://www.dailypress.net/news/local-news/2019/05/nahma-mourns-loss-of-landmark/

Mansfield and the Mine

https://www.mindat.org/loc-123147.html

https://www.findagrave.com/cemetery/2544643/mansfield-mine-memorial

https://usminedisasters.miningquiz.com/saxsewell/mansfield_news_only.htm

I hope you will continue
to follow my journey at

www.lostinmichigan.net


To follow my travels outside of
Michigan you can visit

www.lostinthestates.com

Made in the USA
Monee, IL
19 June 2022